Everybody's Guide
to
Book Collecting

Everybody's Guide to Book Collecting

by

Charlie Lovett

Pictures by
Jonathan Dixon

Write Brain Publishers • Overland Park, Kansas
1993

ISBN 0-9637840-8-8

Library of Congress Catalog Card Number
93-072558

Additional copies of this book may be ordered from the publisher for $9.95, postpaid in the United States.

Write Brain Publishers
10714 West 128th Ct., Suite 201
Overland Park, KS 66213

FIRST EDITION

♻ *This book and all forms & publications of Write Brain Publishers are printed with soy-based ink on recycled paper made from 100% post-consumer waste.*

Table of Contents

Introduction

"Have you *read* all these books?" was perhaps the most frequently asked question during my years running an antiquarian bookshop, and one which I make no attempt to answer in this book. It always made me wonder if the customer with the puzzled look on his face would next approach a sales clerk at a department store and ask "Have you worn all these clothes?"

For nearly ten years I listened to the earnest questions of those venturing into an out-of-print bookshop for the first time and diehard book collectors as well. "Why do people collect books?" "How can I tell what my books are worth?" "Is this a first edition?" "Where did all these books come from?" One question I was not able to answer in the affirmative was, "Is there a concise, inexpensive guide to book collecting available?"

This volume is intended to be such a guide—an affordable book which answers the questions of both novice and experienced collectors in a straightforward manner and guides you through the joys and hazards of book collecting.

Book collecting is a highly individualized pursuit, yet a certain basis of knowledge is needed in order to understand the workings of the out-of-print book world and to ensure the stability of your investment. This book provides that basis.

I welcome those who are just venturing into the world of book collecting. For those whose collections are already well underway I hope this guide will enhance your enjoyment of the books you have bought and those yet to be bought. For long-time collectors and dealers my wish is that this book will explain your habit to your friends and family, and maybe even teach you something new, too.

Nobody can read "all these books," but I hope that by reading this one you may gain a deeper appreciation of all the others.

Everybody's Guide
to
Book Collecting

Why collect books?

Over the years, whole volumes have been written trying to explain the motivations of collectors in general and book collectors in particular. It has been said that there are two types of people in the world—those who collect and those who throw away—and that neither will ever understand the other. If you collect anything, you require no explanation of the obsessive nature of the collector, or the joy he takes in discovering some new trinket which, though of little significance to nearly everyone else on the planet, perfectly fills an empty spot on his shelves. If, on the other hand, the qualities of the collector are an enigma to you, there is little hope of explaining them except to say that, while each is driven by his own personal motives, all are bound together by that ineffable character trait that makes us so inscrutable to those who do not share it. If you, gentle reader, did not have at least a trace of the collector in your mental make up, you would not be reading this book.

There are a few characteristics, however, which set books apart from other collectibles and which might encourage you to exercise your collecting instincts towards them rather than, say, stamps or wine. Most collectibles are cultural artifacts of some description, but through books we can learn more about our culture than through other collectibles, for books are not only objects with intrinsic physical qualities (artwork, craftsmanship, and technological achievement), but they are also storehouses, containing between their covers the accumulated knowledge of humankind. Collected coins, antiques, or china figurines, may teach you many things, but through books you have the potential to expand your horizons without limit.

Unlike many other collectibles, a book can be used by its owner and enjoyed to its fullest without diminishing its value. Even a book that is worth thousands of dollars can be taken off the shelf and used for its originally intended purpose, albeit carefully. A rare book can still be read. Drink a bottle of wine worth thousands or use a rare stamp to mail a letter and you are left with nothing but memories.

Book collecting is not limited to English majors, literati, or tweed-clad intellectuals. If you are interested in Railroads, German Shepherds, Church Architecture, Ant Farms, Cave Painting, Zen Buddhism, Rug Making, or Bulgarian Politics you can add to your enjoyment of that interest through book collecting. There is virtually no topic on which books have not been written, making the possibilities for collecting almost endless. Because of this, books attract a wide variety of collectors from every walk of life.

In addition to all these advantages, books enjoy the qualities of many other collectibles—they can beautify your home, provide a reasonably sound investment, and satisfy your collecting urge; or, from the point of view of the non-collector, they can clutter up the house, deplete your checking account, and make an ordinary person obsessive beyond understanding.

Do I need a lot of money to collect books?

Just as books come on all topics they come in all price ranges, too. Unlike some areas of collecting (fine art, oriental rugs, or fine antiques) book collecting does not necessarily require a deep pocketbook. Even the upper echelons of book collecting are filled with bargains compared to some other fields. Consider that, in 1993, one could purchase a copy of a first edition of Walt Whitman's *Leaves of Grass*, one of the scarcest and most valuable books in the canon of American literature, for $25,000 to $35,000. That same amount invested in, say, oil paintings could not possibly place such a significant work on your walls. Most book collectors appreciate the fact that very few books approach this price range. Thousands of extremely important books may be bought in their first editions for a few hundred dollars or less, and even those are considered big ticket items by most collectors.

Book collections may be built on any budget—you as a collector can set your own parameters. If you wish to collect very fine copies of the first editions of important works of nineteenth and twentieth-century literature, you had best be prepared to spend quite a bit of money; if, on the other hand, you wish to pursue books in a less popular field, you may find yourself adding volumes to your collection for as little as a few dollars each.

What you choose to collect will determine the price range in which you can expect to acquire material. The more popular a collecting field, the higher the prices will be. Fortunately, there is no limit to the fields in which you can collect, and there are thousands of topics which you can pursue at very low prices, since the competition for books in more esoteric categories may be slim. You might well build the world's finest collection of books on an obscure subject without spending more than $20 on any single volume.

Your standards for condition and edition of the books you buy will also affect the cost of your collecting. If you insist that every volume you buy be a first edition in fine condition with its original dust jacket, you will find bargain prices few and far between. If you are collecting only for content, however, and are perfectly satisfied with a paperback reprint or a book lacking its dust jacket, your book collecting will be a surprisingly economical pursuit.

While most collectors do not set a specific budget for book buying, it is important to structure your collecting around your financial constraints. No budget is too small for book collecting, but one must have reasonable expectations about what can be purchased within a particular budget. Someday, though, that $500 book which fills a gaping hole in your collection will show up. You may not eat for a month, but you will probably buy it.

What kind of books should I collect?

One of the wonderful aspects of book collecting is that you can make up all your own rules. You can collect whatever intrigues you, and let your own interests be the guiding force behind your collecting. Few people awake one day and decide to collect books. Most book collectors evolve out of heavy readers and people with a strong interest in a particular field. When you realize that you own a case full of biographies or books on forestry because those subjects interest you, you may decide to pursue collecting more purposefully.

There are several factors to keep in mind when setting the parameters of your collection. The first of these is simply the importance of setting *some* limits to what you will buy. If you are collecting books about tea, will you collect books about the tea trade, tea as a meal, the Boston Tea Party, and copies of *Alice in Wonderland* which illustrate the Mad Tea Party? Without some limits a collection can quickly grow out of hand. Focus is important in collecting, and while you may not wish to collect only books on one topic or by one author, you will find that some sort of focus to your collecting will make it a more rewarding endeavor.

While a broad focus can overwhelm a collector, too narrow a focus may eliminate many books which you would have found exciting additions to your collection. If you are interested in the works of a particular author, don't overlook the possibility of acquiring biographies of that author, literary criticism of his works, and appearances of his pieces in magazines or anthologies. Collectors of a non-fiction topic often find that the addition of novels which focus on that topic rounds out their collections nicely.

Consider the constraints of budget, mentioned in the previous section, when setting limits to your collection. If you have only a few dollars a week to spend on books, you will not get much enjoyment from collecting thirteenth-century illuminated manuscripts. If you are concerned about the stability of your investment in books, you may want to concentrate on a mainstream area such as first editions of literature or Americana in order to ensure that a market will exist should you ever wish to resell your collection.

Within these general guidelines you should collect whatever you want. A book collection should be a reflection of the collector's personality, but most collections are interesting because of a common bond shared by the books. Collections have been built not only of books by a single author or on a single subject but also of books illustrated by a single artist or school of artists, books with similar bindings, books published by the same publisher or in the same year, even books with the same number of pages. In choosing a direction for your collecting, you are limited only by your imagination.

Finding a focus for your collection will not only make it easier for you to decide what books to buy, but also provide you with those thrilling moments when you find a book that fits perfectly into your collection but is not yet on your shelves.

Are there types of books that collectors avoid?

Depending on the focus of your collection, there will be certain categories of books that you avoid, but there are also types of books which most collectors and dealers agree have little or no resale value. This does not mean you should automatically reject such books. If, for instance, you are collecting all the different editions of *Robinson Crusoe*, you may want to obtain book club editions, in spite of their poor quality.

In addition to book club editions, which are discussed below, most serious collectors are inclined to shun books in poor condition, ex-library books, textbooks, older books on popular topics such as health care and business, condensed versions of popular books, family bibles, and out-of-date reference books. Any of these books may potentially have a place in your collection, but you should expect to pay very little for such volumes.

Collectors' opinions about condition vary, but all agree that books in very good or better condition are far preferable to tattered copies, and many will not include inferior copies in their collections. Of course, if there is a particular book you need, and you are only able to find a copy in poor condition, you may want to purchase it, assuming the price is low. You can always replace it if you find a better copy later on.

Ex-library books are those which have been deaccessioned from a library and have library markings, possibly including glued-on plastic covers, pasted-in pockets, and other stamps and labels. Such copies are grouped with poor-condition copies as undesirable unless absolutely necessary.

Other types of books listed above may or may not fit into your collection, but the market for such books is small enough that most dealers will not carry them at all. If you do need, for instance, an old textbook on American Literature to enhance your Hawthorne collection, you may have more luck finding it at a flea market or yard sale than in a bookshop. In any case, don't let an enthusiastic novice convince you that a tattered Bible from 1885 is worth $100—chances are that 50¢ to $1 would be more reasonable.

While collectible books such as first editions in fine condition or important classics in any field are likely to gradually increase in value over the years, book club editions, books in poor condition, and other undesirables will never be worth more than a few dollars.

What is a book club edition?

Book club editions form one of the largest groups of books avoided by most collectors. If you frequently shop at flea markets, thrift shops, or charity book sales, you have probably already seen thousands of book club editions. These books, sold by mail to club members, are generally printed on a lower grade of paper than the regular, or "trade" editions. They are glued into their bindings rather than stitched, and the bindings themselves are often covered with paper rather than cloth. They are avoided by collectors because of this poor standard of production and also because most collectors prefer to acquire a particular book in the first trade edition, which usually precedes the book club edition. Book club editions are easy to identify once you have seen a few. Most have the words "Book Club Edition" printed on the front flap of the dust jacket, but even if the jacket is lacking you will soon recognize book club editions by the quality of the binding and paper.

Some book clubs issue copies of the trade edition of a book in unpriced dust jackets. While these volumes are not shunned as widely as other book club editions, they are still considered less desirable than copies of the regular trade edition of a book. Signs that a book may be from such a club include the absence of a price on the dust jacket, the presence of a book club notice on the jacket flap, and the presence of a small mark or indentation, usually a circle or square, on the bottom right corner of the book's rear cover. Even some books which state "First Edition" on the back of the title page are actually book club editions, so always check for these indicators.

Are subscription series books collectible?

Most books which are issued by subscription, whether through magazine advertisements or direct-mail solicitations, have not demonstrated strong popularity on the collector market. While the first trade edition of a new novel might rise in price 10% or more per year, a similar book published in a subscriber series is not likely to increase its original value as much.

Part of the reason for this difference is a general perception among book collectors that such series are issued for people who do not know much about books or collecting. Whether or not this image is fair, it has colored the lack of interest shown toward these series by the collecting world.

Another reason these series do not increase in value as much as other books is that they have sometimes been oversold to begin with. Books sold in series are often advertised as "limited editions" when, in fact, they are only limited to the number of current subscribers, which is often several thousand. Even if a book is signed by the author, if a collector knows that there are 12,000 other copies signed in the exact same way, he is not likely to pay a high premium for it.

Are paperback books collectible?

Some paperback books are sought by collectors, but the market for these books is an offshoot from the mainstream collectible book market—not as far removed as the comic book market, but still distinctly different. Some speciality dealers handle collectible paperbacks, but you are most likely to find such books in a used bookshop which devotes a section to them.

Paperbacks have their own price guides and their own standards of condition, and while most are worth no more than a few dollars, some can be worth as much as several hundred. The most sought-after paperbacks are first editions of books, especially science fiction, fantasy, and mysteries, which appeared only in paperback. Also prized are the first paperback printings of important works, especially the novels of the thirties and forties which were often published in paperback editions with lurid covers.

What is a first edition and how does it differ from a first printing?

An edition is all the copies of a book printed from a single setting of type; thus a first edition is all the copies of a book printed from the first setting of type. This definition is simple to understand when applied to the days when type was set by hand and when a book had been printed the individual pieces of type were taken out of the press and used on another job. Now, however, type is set on computers, and an entire book can be stored on a single disk and reprinted without being reset. Today, therefore, even books which are reprinted many times are frequently printed over and over from the same setting of type, making them all, technically, first editions.

When a book collector or dealer uses the term "first edition" he is almost always referring to the first printing of the first edition. A printing is all the copies of a book printed in a single run of the press. In other words, if a publisher orders a printer to print 15,000 copies of a new novel and then, several months later, orders another 10,000 copies to be printed without making any changes, the result is a first and second printing of the first edition. To most book collectors, however, only the first printing is considered desirable, and when they use the term "first edition" without qualification it is the first group of 15,000 to which they refer. The term "impression" is used by British dealers and publishers and is synonymous with "printing."

It is possible for copies of a book from a single printing to differ from one another, and there are two terms which are used to describe such variations: state and issue. A separate state of a printing occurs when a change is made during the press run, but all the books are still published simultaneously. For instance, if, after 2000 copies of our first printing of 15,000 copies had been printed, someone discovered a typographical error in the text, the press might be stopped, the error corrected, and the remaining 13,000 copies printed. All the books would then be sent to the publisher for distribution. This scenario would create a first and second state of the first edition. For a collector the first state would be much more desirable. This would hold true even if the first state consisted of 13,000 copies and the second state of 2000, for the collector nearly always prefers the earliest version of a book, even if it is not the rarest. Of course, many collectors are acquisitive enough that they would want examples of both states.

A separate issue of an edition is similar to a separate state, with the exception that it involves the two groups of books being issued by the publisher at two different times. For example, if the dedication page of a book were improperly printed and the mistake not discovered until 10,000 copies of our first edition had been sent to bookstores, the publisher might return the remaining 5000 copies to the printer, have the faulty page cut out and a new page pasted in, and then issue the remaining copies at a later date, creating a first and second issue of the edition. Dust jackets, too, can have different issues or states. The difference between what constitutes an issue and what constitutes a state can be difficult to discern and some dealers use the terms interchangeably. The differences between the various issues and states of an edition are called "points of issue," or just "points," and are described in bibliographies and some price guides.

In some cases, variants of a book have been noted but bibliographers have been unable to determine which variant came first.

Occasionally, variants are even published simultaneously, as in the case of some nineteenth-century books which were available in several colors of binding. In such cases, books will often be described with the notation "no known priority," meaning that there is no way to determine whether or not the issue described is the first.

Why do so many people collect first editions?

There is a scholarly reason for the collecting of first editions. The first edition of a book is likely the one which the author personally saw through the press and therefore the one most closely reflecting the author's intent with regard to both content and appearance. Typographical errors will sometimes creep into later editions, and editors will tamper with the text without the author's permission. For someone wishing to read, as much as possible, what the author actually wrote, a first edition, in the absence of the original manuscript, is essential.

Most collectors, however, are not textual scholars. They collect first editions simply because they were first. Part of the joy of collecting is the mystique of owning an object, whether a book, stamp, or coin, that is, as closely as possible, exactly as it was when first presented to the public. For the book collector this means a first edition in fine condition.

Collecting first editions is especially popular in the fields of literature and poetry, but collectors in all fields generally prefer the first edition of a book to a later one. The collecting of first editions of modern literature is so standard that most later editions are sold simply as used books, not as collectibles.

First editions are not necessarily expensive, though some come with exorbitant prices. The focus of your collection will determine the price you pay for first editions of the books you seek. Many books, especially those in obscure fields or by lesser known authors, are published in only one edition, so even a non-collector interested in reading the work must find a first edition. This can make the price higher than it would be if the book had been reprinted.

What does "first thus" mean?

Book dealers use "first thus" to indicate that a book is the first printing of the described variation, though not a first edition of the title. In some cases, this can be a significant fact which enhances the value of the book. The first printing of a classic work with a new set

of illustrations by a famous artist may be quite valuable. The first edition of a book with a new introduction by a famous critic, or an edition of a text newly revised by the author may also have collectible value. Such editions, however, while important, are nearly always less valuable than the true first edition. Sometimes the denotation "first thus" is best ignored, as book dealers will use it to make a mundane book sound collectible. In any case, it is an expression which cannot be taken at face value—until you know what the "thus" in question is, you cannot accurately judge the book's importance.

What is a first English edition or first American edition?

Most major works of fiction and many works of non-fiction written in English are published in both the United States and the United Kingdom, frequently by different publishers. The English and American editions usually have different artwork on the dust jacket, and sometimes the text may be revised somewhat from one to the other. Dealers usually refer to an edition as the first English or first American edition when it is the first edition published in that country, but not the true first edition. For instance, a novel published in New York in May, then in London in September would have a first edition (the New York edition) and a first English edition (the London edition).

Sometimes English and American editions are issued within a few days of each other, or even simultaneously. Generally, if the

author is American the first edition will be published in America and if he is British the first edition will be published in England. This is not always so, however, and one must consult a bibliography to be certain which edition is the true first. You may be surprised to find that some well-known American novels were published in England a few days or weeks prior to their appearance in the USA. Ernest Hemingway's 1950 novel *Across the River and into the Trees*, for instance, was published in London three days prior to its appearance in New York.

Many collectors of modern novels like to have both English and American editions on their shelves, so dealers will catalogue both, even though one is not the true first edition. The prices of such editions often depend on where they are purchased. A first English edition of a popular novel originally published in America may cost slightly more than the true first if sold in the US where its supply is likely very low.

How can I tell if a book is a first edition?

Every publishing house has its own method of identifying first editions. Many identifying marks and methods were not standardized until the mid-twentieth century or later, so the older a book, the more difficult it may be to identify as a first edition. Even some books which plainly state "First Edition" on the back of the title page are not, in fact, firsts, or at least not first printings. Some publishers identify firsts by printing no notice to the contrary, labelling only second and later printings. Some use a small row of numbers beginning with "1" and drop one for each subsequent printing. Some even have a special logo which adorns only the first edition.

To accurately identify first editions, one must know which publishers use which method, and this is only possible with a reliable reference book. There are two such books currently available—*First Editions: A Guide to Identification*, which gives detailed statements from publishers at various times throughout the past 65 years, and *A Pocket Guide to the Identification of First Editions*, which is more portable but abbreviates the information considerably. One or both of these books is essential to the collector of first editions.

In the case of books printed before publishers had standardized their identification methods, determining the edition of a book can be much more difficult. Often, but not always, if the date on the title page matches the date on the copyright page the book is a first. *The National Union Catalogue* and *British Museum Catalogue*, both massive bibliographic reference works available at most university libraries, are also helpful in researching older books. The best way to identify editions which are questionable is to consult a bibliography of the subject or author. The reference room of your local university library likely has a large collection of bibliographies. A speciality dealer is also a good source of bibliographical reference material as well as personal knowledge. If you are unable to find a particular book described in any bibliography, you may have to leave the question of its edition temporarily unanswered.

What is a bibliography and how do I use one?

"Bibliography" comes from the words "biblio" meaning book and "graph" meaning writing, and so is, literally, a writing about books. An ideal bibliography will include a complete list of books or other published items in its chosen range (for instance all publications by a certain author) with in-depth descriptions of the various editions of each item. Armed with a well-written bibliography, a book collector should have no difficulty distinguishing between first and later editions of a particular work. A bibliography can provide a collector with an idea of what has been published in his field, and can be an excellent source for creating a want list.

There are hundreds, if not thousands, of bibliographies which describe the works of a single author. Bibliographies have also been written on particular subjects, some narrow in focus and others quite broad. Of the more general works, the multi-volume and authoritative *Bibliography of American Literature* is most commonly used by US dealers. Bibliographies tend to be fairly expensive, as they are printed in relatively small press runs, so you may want to seek out a library to use as a source for bibliographies. Many public libraries and most university libraries have excellent collections of bibliographies, which are usually non-circulating reference books.

In the bibliography section you may also find works billing themselves as checklists. Checklists tend to have less complete information than full blown bibliographies, but can still be helpful to the collector. Bibliographies and checklists are not infallible—many are full of errors. They are, however, the best guide a book collector has and as such are invaluable.

Dealers' catalogue entries will often cite the standard bibliography in a particular field, sometimes with the notation that the book described is not listed in that bibliography. "Not in ..." is often used by dealers to imply that a book is so scarce the bibliographer was unable to locate a copy, and this can be a reasonable assumption if the work cited is a thorough and well respected bibliography. If, however, the work in question has a reputation for incompleteness, the fact that a certain book is not included may not necessarily be an indication of rarity. Another possibility is that the dealer may have misunderstood the scope of the work cited. Collectors and dealers should always carefully read the introductions to reference books to avoid any such confusion.

What other reference works might be helpful to me?

Information for book collectors can come from a variety of sources. You may find selected bibliographies in the backs of books already in your collection. Biographies, collections of criticism, and other non-fiction works often contain such bibliographies. These lists can lead to other reference works pertinent to your interest.

In addition to single author bibliographies and subject bibliographies, general bibliographical references are helpful to collectors. Most university libraries have access to the *MLA Bibliography* which, now on CD-ROM, lists millions of articles and books on all academic subjects. The hundreds of volumes of *The National Union Catalogue*, also in most university libraries, describe books in major libraries all over the United States, including the Library of Congress. Though the NUC does not give detailed bibliographical information, it can be extremely useful in determining what books were written by what authors and how widely published those books are.

Book collectors will find valuable information in other more ephemeral sources, too. Dealers' catalogues are an excellent source of information, and frequently include listings for items not mentioned in the standard bibliographies. Catalogues from book auctions and exhibitions can also be valuable, as they will generally give a full description of the books featured. Even a brief mention of your area of interest in a newspaper or magazine article can set you on the path of a book that fits perfectly into your collection.

What factors contribute to the value of a book?

The value of a book, like that of other products, is determined ultimately by supply and demand. A book of obscure eighteenth-century sermons may be extremely scarce, but if no one is interested in it, its value will be negligible. On the other hand, John Updike's first book, relatively common by comparison and published in 1958, is worth over five hundred dollars because the author is highly collected. To see what factors affect the value of a book, therefore, one must examine the factors that affect its supply and demand.

One of the greatest misconceptions among book world neophytes is that old books are scarce and valuable. There is little direct correlation between age and value in books. Mass production techniques were introduced with the coming of the industrial revolution in the nineteenth century. Books with dates in the 1800s are almost never valuable solely because of their age. As one moves back through the centuries, a correlation between value and age may develop—incunabula, or books published before 1500, are always quite valuable, yet there are many books printed in the seventeenth and eighteenth centuries which have little value in spite of their age. Age is most often a factor in a book's value if the book is an early example of its type—an example of the earliest printing in a particular state or region or one of the first books on a particular topic, for instance.

A much more important factor in a book's value is its importance in its particular field. A first edition of one of Shakespeare's plays, for instance, will always be extremely valuable, while a first edition by an obscure Elizabethan author may bring only a modest price. Any book which is of great importance in its field—Darwin's *Origin of the Species*,

Freud's *Interpretation of Dreams*, and other similarly influential titles—will nearly always be valuable in a first edition.

Edition, too, is a factor which deserves careful consideration. The first edition of any title is considered the most desirable by collectors and will therefore be priced the highest. Books which are extremely scarce in the first edition, however, are likely to command strong prices for any early edition. *Alice in Wonderland*, for instance, a book of which only 21 copies of the first edition exist, can be found in several subsequent early editions which range in price from the hundreds to the thousands of dollars.

The publishing and collecting history of every title is unique, and making generalizations about a book's value is no substitute for a careful examination of a particular copy and research into its value.

How important is condition to a book's value?

The condition of a book is the single most important factor in determining its value. Failure to consider a book's condition is the most common cause of overestimating its value. If a price guide gives the value of a book based on the assumption that it is a fine copy in the original dust jacket as $50 and you find a copy which has a worn cover and no jacket, you have not found a $50 book. In fact, you have found a book with little or no appreciable retail value.

Most collectors are only interested in books that are in very good or better condition (see Appendix A for a guide to grading condition). This means that the demand for copies in such condition is high, though the supply is often low. This can cause a great difference in price between books in collectible condition and those which are worn, soiled, or lacking their dust jackets. Unless a book is extremely scarce in very good condition, most collectors will not even consider buying a copy in fair or poor condition. This means that a book which is worth hundreds of dollars in fine condition, may still be worth very little in poor condition. If, however, a book is extraordinarily scarce, and in demand by collectors, copies in any condition might command a high price. Still, fine copies would sell for far more than those in lesser condition.

Why does a dust jacket enhance the value of a book so greatly?

Many novice book collectors are surprised to find that dust jackets are so highly prized in the book world. Also called dust wrappers, dust jackets are the paper wrappers in which most hard bound books are issued. In the field of collectible modern first editions, common books are virtually unsaleable without their dust jackets. Jackets on rarer volumes will usually increase the price by several times, and in some cases jacketless copies may be worth only 1/20 or less of the price of a copy in a fine jacket. A copy of the first edition of *Tarzan of the Apes*, for instance, is worth as much as $30,000 in a dust jacket, but no more than $1500 without one.

Why do people pay so much for a single sheet of paper that is not even attached to the book? Collectors want to purchase books in as close to their original condition as possible. This means books which are clean, crisp, and jacketed. While this is the primary motivation behind the scramble for dust jackets, there are other reasons for their importance.

Frequently dust jackets contain information not published elsewhere. Famous authors are recruited to write promotional copy, or "blurbs," for the backs of jackets, and the rear flap usually includes a photograph and biographical sketch of the author. Sometimes, the jacket is illustrated by a well-known artist or is representative of a particular art movement. While all these factors can add to the interest of a particular jacket, even if none were present, collectors would still be willing to pay a large premium for a jacketed book. They want the dust jacket because it is a part of the book—they would no more buy a book missing a jacket than one missing chapter six.

Most books published before World War I did not have the same type of dust jackets as books published today. Early jackets were plain paper wrappers which were thrown away when the book was sold. Sometimes they included the title or price of the book, but usually little other printed information, and no artwork. Jackets from the pre-World War I period (some dating well back into the nineteenth century) are relatively scarce, but are not considered by collectors to be as essential as later jackets. Since the early jackets were generally only intended to protect the book before it was sold, they are placed by collectors in the same category as prepublication material or publisher's packaging—nice to have, but not essential to the integrity of the book.

Around the end of World War I, however, publishers began to use dust jackets as a marketing tool, and the addition of brightly colored artwork, review quotes, and other information revolutionized the jacket. At the same time, the highly decorated bindings which characterized the Victorian and Edwardian periods disappeared, as publishers found it less expensive to limit cover art to the dust jacket. The modern dust jacket was a result of these developments. Most book collectors prefer to have jackets on any books published after about 1920, though every collector sets his own standards appropriate to his scope and budget.

As with the book itself, the dust jacket's condition is important to collectors. Jackets which are soiled, torn, or even price-clipped (having the book's price neatly cut off of the front flap by a well-intentioned gift giver) are always worth less than clean undamaged jackets.

Do illustrations contribute to a book's value?

The market for illustrated books has traditionally been strong, with finely produced books illustrated by well-known artists leading the way. While the presence of illustrations per se does not necessarily add to the value of a book, books illustrated by famous and admired artists such as Arthur Rackham, Edmund Dulac, Kate Greenaway, and others can command high prices if they are in fine condition. Books illustrated by artists who are not primarily known for their book work, such as Pablo Picasso, Salvador Dali, and Henri Matisse, are also popular with collectors, and their prices are driven up since they appeal to both book and art enthusiasts. Collectors of children's books are especially interested in the quality of illustrations and first editions of picturebooks by illustrators such as Dr. Seuss, Maurice Sendak, and Tasha Tudor are highly prized.

Books with fine illustrated plates from the nineteenth century and earlier are also widely collected, especially when the plates have been colored by hand. Some print dealers will cut plates out of such books and sell them separately as prints. This practice, known as book breaking, is frowned upon by most people in the book world as the blatant destruction of beautiful books for profit. When buying illustrated books, examine volumes carefully to be certain that all the plates are present.

Collectors of illustrated books are often interested in the book as a physical object and a work of art, so condition is extremely important in gauging the value of illustrated books. Private press books with fine bindings and beautifully printed illustrations will always be popular with collectors and therefore command high prices, but a tattered children's book illustrated by an obscure artist may have little or no value.

How can I judge the value of a specific book?

There are many sources which can help determine the value of a particular collectible book. When using any of these guides, read the introduction and take into account how factors such as condition might cause the value of your copy of a book to vary from that listed in the price guide.

There are three basic types of book price guides—those which give prices based on the experience and knowledge of the author, those which give prices based on specific dealer catalogue entries, and those which give prices based on the results of auctions. Of these three, the first is likely to be the best general guide, since the prices listed are not for specific copies of the books and since some extraneous factors that affect catalogue and auction prices are not present. There are many such price guides—some cover specialized areas such as Americana, the Civil War, or children's books; some are devoted to the works of a single author; and some cover collectible books in general. Of this third category, *Collected Books: The Guide to Values* is currently the most widely used. To find out about other more specialized price guides, look in the reference department of your library and watch for advertisements for newly published guides in the various periodicals listed in Appendix C.

The standard price guide based on dealers' catalogues is *Bookman's Price Index*. This hefty work is issued on a regular basis and is often found in the reference section of larger libraries. The volumes of BPI are quite expensive, so you will probably want to use the copies in your library. If you have trouble locating copies, ask at the rare book department of a nearby university library. This is a good source for all types of reference materials on book collecting.

The entries in BPI are based on the catalogues of several dozen dealers in the United States, Canada, and Great Britain. Entries usually include a description of the book's condition and other factors likely to affect the price. Each entry also gives the name of the dealer whose catalogue is cited. This information can be very important, as you will soon find that some dealers (those with high overheads located in big cities or in inflated economies such as the West Coast) tend to have much higher prices than others. A book which sells for $50 at a small roadside shop in rural New England may sell for $150 in an upscale store in Beverly Hills. Geography and economics are just two more factors to consider in estimating the resale value of your books. What BPI does not record is whether the books listed actually sold for the catalogued price. These are asking prices, *not* records of sales.

The results of all major book auctions are recorded each year in *American Book Prices Current*, another thick and expensive volume. Auction records can be sketchy, often excluding information about a book's condition. Auction prices can also be artificially inflated if two wealthy bidders desperately wanted the same book or deflated if a sudden snowstorm kept bidders out of the gallery that day. Nonetheless, checking several volumes of ABPC can give you an idea of the sales history of the book you are researching.

When using either ABPC or BPI to assess value, try to find several citations for your book. This way you can detect a trend in the pricing of that book rather than depending on a single reference which may be affected by factors unknown to you. You will find that these two guides emphasize different types of books. For example, Americana appears at auction (and therefore in ABPC) less often than fine illustrated books.

In addition to published price guides, there are other sources for discovering a book's value. One of these is dealers' catalogues. Once you have been collecting for a while, you will accumulate quite a stockpile of these. Think carefully before discarding old catalogues, as they are a valuable reference tool, and an inexpensive one, too. Again, a library's rare book department will probably have a large collection of dealer catalogues that you can search through. While catalogues have the disadvantages of BPI, they often have the advantage of being limited to specific topics. Sometimes, in the absence of a price guide or bibliography on a certain topic or author, a comprehensive dealer's catalogue will become the standard reference work in that area.

Dealers themselves can also be a good source of pricing information, especially in their area of speciality. While you should never take advantage of a dealer by asking for a free appraisal, you may get a general idea of the price range of books you are looking for by discussing your needs with a dealer. Looking at the prices of books in a dealer's shop can also guide you in valuing a book.

Wherever you get your pricing information, examine your own book carefully to be sure it matches the description in a price guide or catalogue or the book in a bookshop. If the edition is not the same and the condition is not comparable, chances are the price for your book will be quite different.

What if I can't find a price reference anywhere?

In the history of publishing tens of millions of titles have been printed and most of them will not be found in any used book price guide. Price guides, including dealer catalogues and auction records, concentrate on books for which there is an established demand among collectors. Chances are, if the book you have is not listed in any such guide, it is not highly sought after by collectors and therefore worth less than about $50. *American Book Prices Current*, for instance, only lists books which sold for over $50, so the absence of your book in several volumes of that guide may indicate that it is relatively common and inexpensive.

This is not always the case, however. Sometimes a book is scarce enough that it does not often turn up in price guides. Another possibility is that the book has been overlooked by cataloguers as a significant volume. In these cases, you will almost certainly find listings for similar books which can be used to gauge an approximate value for your book. If, for example, you find listings for several other books by the same author, you may be able to estimate where your book fits into the price range of that author's work. Keep in mind that books published early in an author's career tend to be more valuable, since they were usually published in smaller press runs, than those published later. While estimating value based on listings for similar books is better than being left in the dark, it can be quite inaccurate unless you are an expert in the field. If you genuinely believe you have uncovered a book which is valuable, you may want to show it to a dealer who could appraise it for you (for a fee) should the two of you decide that is necessary.

Is a book signed by the author worth more than an unsigned copy?

The simple answer to this question is "Yes." The presence of the author's signature in a book does add to its value. How much the value increases is a much more complex question. In judging the value of a signature a variety of factors must be taken into account, the most important being the stature of the author and his autographing habits.

Even for the inexperienced collector, the first of these factors may be easy to evaluate. Major authors in any field, especially literature, are sought after for their signatures as well as for their first editions. The combination of both means considerable value.

Judging the signing habits of a particular author, however, is a task best left to the specialist. Not until you have been collecting for some time will you begin to have an idea of what authors' books are widely available in signed copies and whose are rarely seen in this state. Some authors, especially local columnists or county historians, may sign the vast majority of their books, for these books are often sold exclusively at signings in local bookstores. The well-known writer J. D. Salinger, on the other hand, is notoriously reclusive and signs almost no books, making the few he does sign quite valuable.

When considering purchasing a recently published book with the author's signature, keep in mind that the signing tour has become a major marketing tool in the publishing industry. Authors travel to major cities across the country and sign hundreds of copies of their books each day for those who wait patiently in line. Obviously, such a vast number of signed copies means that the value added by the signature will not be great.

What is the difference between a signed and inscribed book?

An inscribed copy of a book is one in which the author has written a personal message, not merely his signature. Collectors seek out signed copies of books because they are more intimately associated with the author than unsigned copies. For the same reason, there is more value to inscription copies than to copies which contain only a signature. Many collectors are willing to pay high prices for a copy of a book which contains a warm inscription from the author to a close friend or family member.

Inscription copies escalate in value according to the length of the inscription and the significance of the author's relationship to the recipient. A book inscribed to someone who cannot be identified by researching the author's life will be worth less than one inscribed to his wife, mother, editor, English teacher, or best friend. The copy of *Walden* that Thoreau inscribed to Emerson and other similarly famous inscription copies will always be tremendously valuable. The ultimate inscription copy of any book is usually the dedication copy. This is the copy of the book which the author inscribes to the person to whom the book is dedicated.

You will often see the term "presentation copy" used to describe an inscribed copy of a book. This should mean that the book was a gift from the author. Whether the author or the recipient provided a book for inscription can be difficult to ascertain, however. In the absence of other evidence, books are often catalogued as presentation copies based on the wording of their inscriptions.

What is an association copy?

An association copy has some special association with the author or some other well-known person. Presentation and inscription copies are sometimes referred to as association copies because of their links to the author, but there are other types of associations as well.

Any of the following might legitimately be described as an association copy: A book signed by a famous author, a book inscribed by a close relative or friend of the author, a book inscribed by its illustrator, or a book with the margin comments of a famous person or which came from the library of an important figure. Since "association copy" is an umbrella term, different dealers will use it in different ways, but always with the implication that the association will add value to the book. In some cases the book would have little or no value without the association and the association accounts for the entire price.

How can I tell if a book is from a famous person's library?

Books that once belonged to the author or other important figure are described as "Ex Libris" (not to be confused with "ex-library") in dealers' catalogues. The provenance, or history of ownership, of these books may be substantiated by a bookplate, the signature of the owner, or accompanying documentation.

Many collectors who pursue the works of a particular author like to have books from that author's personal library in their collection, as well as copies of that author's works from the libraries of other notables. Ownership by any famous person will add to the value of a book, but if the person is somehow tied to the book, the value is further increased. A book which inspired T. S. Eliot to write a passage of poetry, or provided background material for a William Styron novel, will be of significant value if it can be shown to have belonged to the person in question.

How can I authenticate an author's signature?

While there are autograph guidebooks which include facsimiles of famous signatures, there is no substitute for consulting with an expert on this issue. Forgery is only rarely an issue in the world of books because forging an entire book would be so expensive and complicated. Forging an autograph or written document, however, can be done with a little expertise and effort, and, if successful, can be quite profitable. For this reason, always consult with a dealer specializing in autographs before investing a large sum in such materials. A small consultation or appraisal fee will be more than compensated for by the safety of your investment.

Are limited editions valuable?

Like so many other terms in the book world, "limited edition" has many meanings. While a limited edition is often much more valuable than an ordinary copy of a book, you must be sure you know all the facts about such an edition before making a judgement as to its value.

Strictly speaking, all books are limited editions, for they are printed in a finite number of copies, but in the book world the term usually refers to one of three types of books. The first is books which bear a printed notice, on the back of the title page or on a separate page in the front or rear of the book, stating "Limited Edition," without giving any additional information. These books are rarely worth more than they would be without such a notice. If a publisher fails to state how many copies the edition is limited to, you can be almost certain that it is merely limited to the number of copies he thought could be sold and that the term was added to the book to try to make an ordinary edition seem special.

The second type of limited edition is the publishers' limited edition. Such an edition is usually brought out just before or simultaneous with the trade edition of a book by a well-known author. When an author has established himself as a major talent, his publisher will sometimes issue his new book in a limited edition. These editions are usually somewhat nicer than the trade edition. Sometimes they are bound in a special binding and/or housed in a slipcase, an open-ended box covered in paper or cloth into which the book can be slipped. In the front or rear of the book is a colophon page which states how many copies are in the edition and often includes the author's signature.

Many limited editions include a number in each copy of the book. The books are numbered sequentially from one to the number of limitation. Like all limited editions, publishers' limited editions are more valuable the smaller the limitation is. An edition of 2000 copies, for instance, may never be worth more than $50–$100 unless the author's works are highly sought after by collectors. On the other hand, an edition of 250 copies may soon be worth several times its original asking price if there are hundreds of people collecting the works of that author. Publishers' limited editions are usually printed in runs of 200–2000 copies, with the average being around 500.

The third major category of limited editions is those published by small or speciality presses. These cover a vast array of books from the beautifully re-illustrated classics of the Limited Editions Club, to newly published works of poetry and literature issued by the many private presses in this country and abroad. The value of these editions depends on a variety of factors, especially the popularity of the author or illustrator, the size of the edition, and the quality of production. Again, the presence of the author's signature on the edition will enhance its value.

Limited editions are published primarily for book collectors, not for the general public. When collecting limited editions, you are not so much collecting pieces of popular culture as items which were manufactured to be collected. While most book collectors believe that there is more intrinsic value in a limited edition book than in manufactured collectors' items in other fields, the distinction between books made to be read and those made to be collected is important to some. Nonetheless, many limited editions are fine examples of bookmaking, exhibiting qualities too often lacking from trade books. Because limited editions are made to be cherished, collectors have high standards for their condition. Even more than in other types of books, the value of a limited edition will drop sharply if its condition is much below fine.

Is one number on a limited edition more valuable than another?

Many limited edition books are individually numbered, and some collectors like to pursue copies with a particular number. The number "1" book is considered the most desirable by some, perhaps because it is often retained by the publisher, so that copy is sometimes worth a bit more than others.. In general, though, the number of a copy is not a contributing factor to its value.

Some editions are limited to a certain number of copies for sale and a certain number of copies for private distribution. This is often the case with books published by small or private presses. Sometimes the copies for private distribution are numbered differently, marked with letters instead of numbers, or specially bound. These copies are given by the publisher and the author to friends and colleagues. Such special copies are worth more than copies intended for public sale, though how much more depends on the popularity of the author and the nature of the differences between the two issues.

What is a private press?

Private presses are small publishers whose books are issued in small editions and are rarely available through new book stores. Some private presses sell books by subscription, while others market their publications directly through the collectible book market. Private press books are usually of a very high quality and are often hand printed and bound. Most operators of private presses are more interested in producing beautiful books than in generating large profits and books from private presses are often works of art in themselves. Private press books should not be confused with privately printed books. The latter are any books which were published for private distribution only and were not intended for public sale. Such books run the gamut from shoddily produced vanity books to highly important and collectible items.

Some book dealers specialize in private press books and other examples of fine printing, and you will see many examples of such books in the collectible marketplace. With the increasing tendency of some major publishers to shirk production quality in favor of higher profits, private presses are shouldering more of the responsibility for producing books whose physical attributes are worthy of their content, and which, with care, will last for centuries to come.

What is an advance copy?

Advance copies of a book are copies distributed by the publisher in advance of the book's publication to book reviewers and other potential sources of publicity. Advance copies may take several forms, the two most common being advance proof copies and advance review copies.

Advance proof copies are generally made up from the typeset pages of the book before they have been subjected to their final proofreading. Most proof copies are bound in plain paper wrappers which bear the title of the book and the publication date. Sometimes, authors make significant changes in the text between the time proof copies are distributed and publication of the book. For this reason such copies may be of interest to scholars as well as collectors. For collectors who seek out the earliest version of a book they can find, the proof copy represents a step prior to the first edition. The number of proof copies distributed by a publisher varies widely from book to book, but today some publishers will send out as many as several hundred. Proof copies for recent books, therefore, are not extremely rare, but they are scarcer than the published versions of the books and therefore more expensive. Proof copies for older books are likely to be rarer and, in the case of important works, can be quite valuable.

Advance review copies are copies of the published book, identical to those sold in bookstores, which are sent out in advance of the publication date to reviewers. Review copies generally contain a slip of paper stating the date of publication and may be accompanied by other promotional materials. Some will be stamped on the endpaper or title page "Review Copy Not For Sale." Since review copies do not differ substantially from the published first edition of a book, they are generally not much more expensive. However, because of collectors' interest in special copies of a book, as well as copies which were distributed as early as possible, review copies are usually priced a bit higher than regular first editions.

Some publishers issue advance reading copies of a book. These copies are generally made up from the printed pages of the first edition bound in a paper binding rather than a hard cover. At first glance, an advance reading copy may look like an oversized paperback edition of the book, and they sometimes carry no identifying marks. These copies may be sent to reviewers and are also made up to be distributed to wholesalers and bookstore owners at the American Booksellers Association annual convention. They are usually printed in fairly large numbers and are rarely worth much more than the first edition.

In addition to these more common types of advance copies, you may encounter other forms. For various reasons, publishers may distribute the unbound pages of a book wrapped in a sample dust jacket, or may issue proof copies in a plastic spiral binder.

Most books go through a variety of printed stages before they reach their final form. While most of these interim formats are for publishers' in-house use only—proofreading by the author and editors, etc.—some of these copies do surface on the collectible book market. Such in-house copies are usually printed in very small numbers, frequently less than a dozen or so, and can be quite valuable. The primary stages between a manuscript and a published book are long galleys, which contain the typeset text of the book on long strips of paper, and page proofs, which contain the typeset text as it will appear in the book, broken into separately numbered pages. Galleys and page proofs are printed on one side of a page only. Some printers also send publishers blue-line proofs, which are unbound pages printed in blue ink.

Some collectors eschew advance materials all together, preferring to collect books rather than piles of paper or publicity items. Others, however, find that advance material can take them one step closer to the creative process of the author and delight in adding it to their collection.

Do book dealers sell manuscripts and autograph material?

If collecting advance copies represents a step closer to the author, the logical next step would be the acquisition of a book's original manuscript. While finding the complete original manuscript of a book offered for sale is uncommon, some do appear, albeit at fairly high prices. The days of longhand manuscripts or even piles of pages battered out on a manual typewriter are nearly over. Most manuscripts produced today are computer printouts, and cannot be guaranteed unique as in the past. Still, whatever its physical form, the

original manuscript of a favorite book is something many collectors
would pay handsomely for.

Much more common on the market, and much less expensive, are
smaller pieces of autograph material from famous authors. The most
common form of such material is the letter, sometimes typed, and
sometimes written longhand, or, in autograph parlance, "holograph."
Many dealers' catalogues include a selection of autograph letters and
there are dealers who specialize in autograph material of famous
people in all fields. The prices of such letters vary greatly, depending
on the importance of the writer, the importance of the letter (a
marriage proposal beats out a thank you note any day), and the
scarcity of material by that particular writer. You may be able to
acquire autograph letters by your favorite author for less than $100
each, or they may cost you several thousand.

While the cost of collecting letters or manuscripts can be high,
many collectors find that representative pieces of original material
from a favorite author add a new dimension to their collection.

Do collectors collect things other than books?

Many book collectors are interested in a particular field that has
produced collectibles other than books. For instance, a collector of art
books might collect prints, museum catalogues, and even original
works of art. Some book dealers handle other sorts of printed material
besides books, and much of this material is sought after by book
collectors.

One term you will hear referring to such material is "ephemera."
Ephemera means, literally, things which were not intended to last.
Dealers use the term to refer to a wide variety of materials, including
vintage advertising, posters, playbills, letters, stock certificates, magazines, newspapers, scrapbooks, photographs, and much more.

Some non-book items which may fit into a book collection have
their own networks of dealers separate from the book world. Film
posters, for instance, have recently become extremely popular collectibles and a network of dealers and trade publications has devel-
oped to serve the needs of poster collectors. Some book collectors
who seek all the works of a particular author may want the original
poster from a film version of the author's work or a videotape of the
movie.

Children's book collectors sometimes find themselves in antique
toy stores buying toys or games based on the characters in their

favorite books, or at art galleries bidding on original artwork for book illustrations. Comic book versions of books in your collection may be found at your local comic book store.

The type of non-book materials which can be included in your collection is limited only by your choice of subject and your own imagination.

Should I save ephemera inserted in old books?

Often you may find that a previous owner has inserted a variety of material in a copy of an old book. Usually such material is related to the book or its author—newspaper reviews, obituaries, or feature articles. Such material can add to your knowledge of the book and its author, and should not be thrown away. Between the pages of a book, however, is not the best place to store it. Newspaper, because of its high acidic content, will badly stain book pages over a period of time, and other materials can both stain pages and put unnecessary pressure on a book's binding. If you acquire a book with inserted material, remove the material immediately and place it in an acid free storage envelope or file folder. Label the envelope or folder with the name of the book and store it with other records related to your collection. This will help preserve both the ephemeral material and the book itself.

What is the difference between secondhand, collectible, and antiquarian?

The term "secondhand" denotes books which have had at least one previous owner and which are being sold merely for their content, not for their rarity or appeal to collectors. These books are usually priced in the $1–$25 range, depending on condition, supply and demand, size, and the location and overhead of the dealer selling them.

Collectible books are those whose value is enhanced by their appeal to collectors. These books are priced higher than secondhand books and their price is much more greatly affected by factors such as condition, edition, and the presence of a dust jacket. While an individual can choose to collect any type of book, the book world labels a book collectible if there is an established market for it or similar titles among book collectors.

"Antiquarian" is frequently used in the book world and means many thing to many people. Most dealers use it interchangeably with "collectible." Many dealers who advertise antiquarian books sell modern first editions and other recently published volumes. You may reasonably expect, however, that a dealer who purports to be an antiquarian bookseller deals in collectible books, at least some of which are from the nineteenth century or earlier.

What does "out of print" mean?

A book is out of print if copies may no longer be obtained from its publisher or a new book distributor. Books which are currently available from these sources are in print. At any time there may be hundreds of thousands of titles in print, so just because a book is not on the shelves of your local new book store does not mean it is out of print. Most new book stores and libraries have a reference book titled *Books In Print* which is ostensibly a listing of all books currently in print in the United States arranged by title, author, and subject.

While *Books In Print* is the best guide to what is in print, it is not 100% accurate. Publishers provide information to *Books In Print* and will sometimes list books that have not yet been published or books which have gone out of print, to see if enough orders are generated to justify printing those titles. Some publishers provide incomplete information on their currently available titles, and some smaller publishing houses and private presses choose not to be listed at all. Since *Books In Print* is only published annually, many books go in and out of print between editions. Still, *Books In Print* is a fairly good guide to the current offerings of American publishers. Most full service new book stores should be able to order copies of books listed in *Books In*

Print for you. Some chain stores, however, buy all their books from distributing companies that frequently do not handle titles from smaller publishers. An established independent new book store is often your best source for special orders of books which have not yet gone out of print.

Many secondhand and collectible dealers will use the term "out-of-print" to describe their stock. This does not necessarily mean that every title in the shop is no longer in print. A speciality dealer may have a first edition of *Gone With the Wind* in his stock, though this is a title that is still available through the new book market. In the book world "out-of-print" is often used as an umbrella term and a nicer way of saying "secondhand."

What is a remainder?

When a publisher decides he has made as much profit as possible from a particular title and he wants to put it out of print, he will sometimes remainder the copies left in the warehouse. This means he will sell his entire stock to a wholesaler at a very low price—as little as 5–10% of the cover price. The wholesaler then sells large quantities of the books to bookstores and discount stores who offer the books on their sale tables. The low price is passed on to the customers, and the books usually retail for 50% of the original price or less.

Sometimes collectors can find first editions of popular novels and other items which might fit their collection at remainder tables. When buying remainders, however, examine the books carefully.

Such copies are often damaged in their bulk shipping and may have torn dust jackets or bumped corners. Many remainders also have a mark, from either a publisher's stamp or a felt marker, on the top or bottom edge of the pages. Though such a mark will not completely destroy the value of a collectible book, it will effect that book's future worth, and most collectors prefer to avoid marked remainders.

What should I know about buying new books?

Although book collectors do much of their purchasing from secondhand or antiquarian dealers, you will doubtless haunt new bookstores as well, looking for recent titles which belong in your collection. Shopping carefully for new books is a task which may be richly rewarded.

Different bookstores stock different titles, and you should become familiar with the bookstores in your area. Independent bookstores often stock obscure titles which are not on the shelves of the chain stores. Patronizing your local independent bookstores ensures that they can continue to offer the kind of eclectic and esoteric stock that will never make it to the mall.

When purchasing a new book, first find an undamaged copy. Check for tears or abrasions on the dust jacket or other damage. Try to find a copy without any price stickers. If you do buy a copy with a price sticker, remove it carefully as soon as you get home.

Next, check to see if the book is a first printing. Sometimes, stores will display more than one printing of a book at a time, and since the firsts probably arrived at the store earlier than the later printings they are often at the bottom of the stack or the back of the shelf.

Finally, be aware of special events at your local bookstores. Many stores sponsor readings and signings by famous authors who are promoting recent books, and you should not miss out on an opportunity to have a book for your collection personally inscribed to you by the author.

Where can I buy secondhand and collectible books?

There are a variety of sources for secondhand books and which you use necessarily depends on what type of books you collect. If your primary interest is not collectible but merely secondhand books, you may find that thrift stores, yard sales, and flea markets are good sources. Don't expect to find hidden rarities at bargain basement prices, though—it does happen but not often. Public libraries frequently conduct sales of donated and deaccessioned books and this can be another source of inexpensive volumes. You can anticipate that books from all these sources will rarely be in collectible condition, but they may fill your particular needs.

A step up from the flea market is your local used book shop. These shops generally carry secondhand copies of both hardbacks and paperbacks with stock covering many categories. There is great variety among used book stores, but these establishments are marketing their goods primarily to readers, not collectors, and the stock is chosen and priced accordingly. Some of these shops include an antiquarian section with higher priced collectibles, but the primary emphasis is on readable books at reasonable prices. Such stores are often found near college campuses where there is a large population that craves books but has little extra money.

At the upper end of the retail scale, in both price and quality of stock, is the antiquarian or specialized book dealer. These dealers sometimes operate shops, but often do most of their dealing via mail order catalogues and antiquarian bookfairs. Speciality dealers sell books to collectors, rare book libraries, and other dealers. The books are priced for their value in this market and condition is a key factor in pricing and in the dealer's desire to handle a particular volume.

Finally, many large auction houses, especially in New York and London, have sales of collectible books. Because of the cost of offering objects at auction, these books tend to be priced in the hundreds of dollars and above, or else grouped in lots that will yield such prices. Some smaller auction houses specializing in books do offer lots in the $50–$100 range, though. Most books at auction are bought by dealers, either at the request of a specific client or for general stock.

How can I locate secondhand bookshops?

A logical first step in the search for bookshops is your local yellow pages under the heading "Book Dealers—Used and Rare." Secondhand bookshops are often off the beaten path, so there may be some in your town that you are not aware of. If not, try the yellow pages for the nearest major metropolitan area or college town.

Another good starting place is *American Book Trade Directory*. Most large libraries keep this annually updated reference work. Here you will find a listing of both a new and used book stores across the

United States. While the listing for secondhand dealers is by no means comprehensive, it can be a good start. Speciality dealer guides, such as those described in Appendix C, also list dealers with open shops.

Once you find a dealer, ask him about other shops or dealers in the area. In many states, groups of dealers get together to publish a brochure listing all the bookshops in the area. The secondhand book world is a tight-knit community, and once you have found a bookshop, a talk with the proprietor will almost certainly lead you to others.

What services can I expect from a secondhand bookshop?

In addition to selling secondhand books, many bookshops offer related services which can be useful to the collector. The most common of these is the out-of-print search service, which is described more fully below. Some dealers maintain a file of customers' general wants so that you can be contacted if books which may interest you are acquired by the store. Because bookshops are often run by people interested in all aspects of the book world, you will sometimes find stores which offer book binding and repair, restoration of papers and documents, or even publishing services, but if your local bookshop does not provide such services the proprietor may be able to refer you to a company which does.

Virtually all secondhand shops buy old books directly from individuals. If you have books to sell you may find shops which offer a variety of options, including outright purchase, consignment, or trading books for store credit. Phone ahead before taking books to a shop to offer them for sale. The proprietor will be able to tell you what types of books he buys, and may save you the trouble of bringing in books which will not interest him.

Most bookstores which offer services above and beyond the buying and selling of books maintain a mailing list to keep their customers informed of such services and of special events, such as readings or book signings, sponsored by the store. Get on the mailing list of your local bookshop so you don't miss out on the opportunities it affords.

What is an out-of-print search service?

Many bookshops advertise that they will search for specific out-of-print titles for their customers. An out-of-print search service can be invaluable in tracking down a particular book which interests you.

Some bookshops provide the service for free, while others charge a small fee. As with any service, you get what you pay for, and free searches are subsidized by higher prices on located books. Before using any search service, ask the dealer to explain how he searches for books.

Some search services are really no more than customer want files. The dealer records the book you are looking for, then, if he happens to come across a copy, he calls you. Most search services include placing an advertisement in the trade journal of the out-of-print book world, *AB Bookman's Weekly*. The AB consists primarily of lengthy advertisements of books for sale and books wanted, and many dealers conduct most of their business through its pages. If you want to have a reasonable chance of finding the book you are looking for as quickly as possible, you should be sure that it will be advertised in the AB.

More and more companies are beginning to offer computer databases which match books wanted with books for sale, and this method of searching for out-of-print books may one day replace the AB. It has not yet become the standard for the industry, however, and without the majority of active dealers on line, it will not do so.

There are several things to be aware of when a dealer is conducting an out-of-print search for you. First, be patient. Dealers wait to accumulate a reasonable number of customer requests before placing an advertisement in the AB, and the lag time between a dealer's sending in the advertisement and its actual publication is about three weeks. Following that, the dealer must wait for other dealers to respond to his advertisement, a process that often continues for several weeks. In order to expedite a book search, tell the dealer exactly how to get in touch with you, and return any phone calls from him as soon as possible.

Second, don't assume that because you are using a professional search service you will find the book. If the book you are searching for is fairly common, the dealer may receive several quotes from other dealers offering copies for sale. In this case, he will be able to offer you a choice of different copies. Sometimes the dealer will receive only a single quote and if you want the book you will have no choice of price or condition. In many cases, though, the advertisement will draw no response. Some dealers will run the advertisement again several weeks later, or give you the option of paying to have it run on a continuing basis, but many books simply cannot be found. The most difficult books to find through an out-of-print search are those printed in small press runs for a very limited audience. These include genealogies, county histories, and other highly specialized works. Some children's books are also very difficult to find, due to supply and demand. Few children's books survive their initial owners, yet nearly everyone would like a copy of their favorite childhood book.

Finally, books found through a search service tend to be more expensive than those you might find on the shelves of your local bookshop. There are several reasons for this, the main one being that the dealer who sells the book to you must buy it from another dealer, whose price must include packing and shipping costs. Also, there is considerable labor involved in selling a book through a search service. Descriptions of books from other dealers must be sorted and compared, phone calls must be made to customers (or, more often than not, to unanswered phones or answering machines), orders must be placed, checks cut, packages unwrapped, and more phone calls placed to tell the customer that the book has finally arrived. If you are seriously interested in owning a copy of a particular book, you probably won't balk at paying $25–$35 for a copy which, if you happened to be lucky enough to find it on your own, might only cost $10, but you should be aware that search books are not bargains. In spite of the high costs of the books, dealers rarely make much profit on search services due to the time and effort put into them. Search services are usually operated as a way to get customers into a bookshop for the first time.

An out-of-print search service that employs the pages of the AB, perhaps in combination with a computer matching service and an in-store want file, is the best possible way to find a copy of a particular out-of-print title, but that does not mean it will always work or that the book will come cheap.

Where do bookshops get all their books?

Unlike new bookstores and most other retail establishments, secondhand bookstores cannot merely order stock from a distributor or manufacturer and then reorder when that stock begins to run low. Obtaining quality books to fill shelves is the biggest challenge facing the proprietor of a secondhand bookshop.

Dealers buy books from customers who bring in the results of spring cleaning, people who are moving into smaller houses, book reviewers who receive unsolicited copies of new books from publishers, and collectors who have lost interest in a field or have decided to use their books to generate some cash. Purchases from individuals make up a large portion of most dealers' inventory. Another major source of books is estate sales and auctions. When someone dies leaving a houseful of books, the local book dealer is usually contacted. Dealers may also search for stock at library and charity book sales, at auction houses, and in the stock of other dealers.

The best sources for any dealer will depend on the type of books he sells, his standards of condition, and the amount of space he has to store excess stock. The constant treasure hunt for new stock is what attracts some people to the out-of-print book business and drives others from it.

Are bookshop prices firm?

As in any independently operated business, the prices in a secondhand bookshop are set by the proprietor. Many customers who wouldn't dream of haggling over the price of a dress in a department store are inclined to ask the owner of a bookshop if he can "do any better." While every bookshop has its own policies regarding prices, most dealers put what they consider fair and reasonable prices on their books. That does not always mean there is no room for negotiation, but if you are a serious collector and wish to be remembered when the dealer obtains some rare gem you have been longing for, it is in your own best interest not to be known as a haggler.

If you feel that a particular book is overpriced in comparison with the rest of a store's stock, politely enquire about it. After all, dealers cannot know everything, and it is possible that the price is inadvertently out of line. On the other hand, dealers obtain books from a variety of sources, and while they may pass savings along to the customer when they buy stock at a bargain price, they may be forced to charge extra for books that were purchased from other dealers or through auction houses. The best tactic is to be cautious and polite in negotiating prices. If, when you ask a dealer if his prices are firm, he replies "yes," let the matter drop and know in the future that the price he puts on a book is his best price and one which he considers fair.

How can I find a dealer who specializes in books in my field of interest ?

Many dealers in collectible books do not maintain open shops, so you may not uncover them in your search for bookshops. Once you start collecting, however, you will certainly want to seek out such dealers.

There are many sources which can lead you to dealers, especially to those specializing in a particular type of book. The particulars of these sources are given in Appendix C. The Antiquarian Booksellers' Association of America has over 400 members and their membership directory is arranged both geographically and by speciality. This association is most beneficial to dealers in the New York area and to those who wish to participate in major antiquarian bookfairs, so do not assume that a dealer is disreputable simply because he does not appear in this directory. ABAA dealers tend to be at the high end of the out-of-print book spectrum, selling to collectors and rare book libraries and handling fairly expensive books. They also tend to be knowledgeable in their field and reputable in their dealings.

AB Bookman's Weekly, the trade journal of the secondhand book business, publishes a yearbook which includes a directory of dealers as well as advertisements for dealers and other book related services. Dealers must pay to be listed in this directory, so it, too, is far from comprehensive. It is also arranged by both location and speciality so can be helpful to the neophyte collector. Your local bookseller may be able to lend you a copy of this trade directory, or you may find a copy at the reference desk of your local library.

American Book Trade Directory, an annually updated reference book, contains listings for specialized dealers, as does *Buy Books Where, Sell Books Where*, an oversized paperback updated every 2 years and containing listings for over 2000 out-of-print dealers. The author and subject speciality section of *Buy Books Where, Sell Books Where* is highly detailed and extremely useful.

Why should I want to find a specialized dealer; wouldn't a general bookshop be cheaper?

It is true that dealers who specialize in a specific area tend to have higher prices than general bookshops, but you will find that the additional services and high quality of merchandise available from a reputable specialist will more than offset this price difference if you are a serious collector. A specialist has devoted his career to accumulating knowledge of the books in his field. He will be aware of bibliographical intricacies and points of issue unfamiliar to a generalist. Sometimes, for instance, a general bookshop will sell a book as a first edition when it is not. This is rarely intentional, but no dealer can know everything about every book, and the generalist is much more likely to make such an inadvertent mistake that the specialist.

A specialist is also more able to provide you with rare material in your area. When a collector or other client is interested in selling rare, expensive, or important material, he is much more likely to sell it to a specialist—someone who knows exactly what the material is worth and who can afford to pay a high price since he can sell such merchandise quickly.

While the places you buy your books are necessarily determined by the type of books you collect, and while you will probably always want to pay frequent visits to your local out-of-print shop, if you are serious about collecting in a limited area it would behoove you to consult one or more specialists in that area to assist you.

How can I conduct business with a specialized dealer far from home?

Many specialized dealers do not maintain open shops, but conduct the majority of their business through the mail, by telephone, and by fax machine. For this reason, you can be a regular customer whether you live three miles or three thousand miles away. Once you have found the name and address of a dealer whose stock might interest you, write a letter of introduction. Explain your area of interest and include a list of your current wants if you have one. Ask to be put on the dealer's mailing list and ask if there is a charge for receiving catalogues. Most dealers provide catalogues free to regular purchasers, but, because of the high cost of printing and mailing, they appreciate some small compensation from new collectors unknown to them.

When conducting business with a dealer through the mail, make sure you know what his terms of sale are. Most dealers will allow you to return merchandise within a reasonable period of time, and this policy allows you to inspect the books you have ordered and make sure they are as described in the catalogue. If you do decide, for any reason, to return a book, notify the dealer immediately, so that he may offer the book to another client. Pack the book carefully, using the same packing material which the dealer used to send the book to you. Such courtesies are appreciated and will keep you in the dealer's good graces.

Many superb books are sold without ever being listed in a dealer's catalogue. Once you, your collection, and your wants are known to

a dealer, he may let you know of books he acquires before he lists them publicly. If you have cultivated a friendly and professional relationship with the dealer (paying your bills promptly is one thing that always helps), you are likely to buy some superb items through such private quotes.

How can I buy books at auction?

Many large auction houses conduct sales of rare books, and some smaller houses specialize in auctioning books. Addresses for auction houses offering books are listed in both *American Book Trade Directory* and *American Book Prices Current*. Auction houses will advertise upcoming sales in periodicals of interest to book dealers and collectors. Most auction houses maintain a mailing list and can inform you by mail of upcoming sales. You can subscribe to the catalogues of auction houses, but this can be expensive, especially for the larger houses. Since book auctions often focus on a specific topic, a more economical approach is to order only catalogues for sales that interest you.

Once you have looked over an auction catalogue and decided which lots you would like to bid on, you have several options. You can complete the bid sheet included in the catalogue and mail it to the auction house, go to the sale and bid in person, telephone the house during the sale and bid over the phone, or have a dealer who will be present at the sale represent you. Carefully read the terms in the front of the auction catalogue to see which of these bidding techniques can

be used at the sale in question and what other bidding rules are in place at that house.

Bidding by mail is a good way to keep from spending more than you can afford. Frequently first time auction goers get caught up in the spirit of the bidding and spend more than they intended. The bid you mail to the auction house is the maximum amount you are willing to bid—you may acquire the item for less if no one is bidding against you.

Attending the auction in person or over the phone can be exciting, but you must set limits for yourself. If you decide ahead of time exactly how much you are willing to pay for a particular item and then stop your bidding at that point, you can avoid the danger of overspending in the excitement of the auction.

If you are especially eager to obtain a particular item, it is worthwhile to retain the services of a dealer experienced in auction bidding to represent you. A well-known dealer is more likely to intimidate the competition than an individual, and he will know a variety of tricks to give your bid the best chance for success.

However you bid, the price you pay will be the hammer price (*i.e.* the amount of your winning bid) plus a premium added by the auction house. This premium is usually 10%. If a dealer is representing you, he generally will add another 10%, though his commission may vary depending on how expensive the item is.

Buying books at auction can be exciting, and many of the finest books on the market are sold in this way. As with any other type of

buying, however, careful planning and sound thinking will always
pay off in the long run.

What is an antiquarian bookfair like?

If you are interested in collectible books, sooner or later you will
want to attend an antiquarian bookfair. Some collectors love the
crowded, excited atmosphere of bookfairs, while others shy away
from it, but you should attend at least one.

Antiquarian bookfairs are gatherings of numerous dealers (any-
where from a few dozen to a few hundred) in a single venue. Each
dealer has a booth where he displays his books for sale. A typical
bookfair will have everything from early printed books to modern first
editions to collectible children's books and much more. A bookfair
can be a great place to search for dealers whose specialities interest
you, to compare the price and quality of different dealers' stock, and
to come face to face with dealers with whom you have done mail order
business. It is also a wonderful place to see *lots* of books!

Most antiquarian bookfairs in this country are held in major cities
or in the Northeast, so you may need to plan some travelling depending on where you live. Some of the biggest fairs are held in Boston,
New York, San Francisco, and Los Angeles. Some bookfairs are
sponsored by the Antiquarian Bookman's Association of America,
while others are sponsored by libraries or local groups of dealers.
Schedules of fairs sponsored by the ABAA are available from that
organization upon request. A more complete schedule of bookfairs is
published in every issue of *AB Bookman's Weekly*, copies of which may
be available at your local library or secondhand bookshop.

How can I care for my book collection?

There are two essential rules of book repair and care—remember
that books are comfortable when you are and never do anything that
cannot be undone. Keeping books at a temperature and humidity
that are comfortable to you (60°–70° F and about 50% humidity) will
help ensure their safety.

One of the biggest household enemies of books is water. A book
exposed to excessive dampness is certain to grow mold and mildew.
If this happens, do not clean the book with bread or corn starch as is
sometimes recommended. These vegetable based items will only act
as bait for another major book enemy—insects. To rid a book of
mildew, put it in a warm, dry place with the pages slightly spread apart

and leave it until it is quite dry—several days at least. Then take a clean dry cloth and simply wipe away the dry mildew.

Almost as bad as too much moisture is not enough. Books left in dry places can experience cracked or bowed bindings and other damage, especially if they are leatherbound.

Direct sunlight is harmful to books, especially those with dust jackets. In the sunlight, colors will fade from the jackets in just a few months. While ultraviolet screening glass in your windows or storm windows will slow this process, placing books in areas which receive little or no direct sunlight is preferable. An area lit by incandescent light is best for books, though florescent lights do little damage if they are sleeved in ultraviolet filters.

The best place to store books is on shelves—not in boxes and definitely not in your attic or basement. Books should not be packed too tightly or too loosely. Oversized books, especially thick ones, should be stored flat to avoid stress to the binding. To minimize the effect of pollutants on your books, ensure that your library is a no-smoking area and regularly change the filters in your heating and cooling system. Do everything possible to keep insects and other pests away from your books. Storing books in glass fronted book cases reduces exposure to light, dust, and other pollutants. Dust your books lightly every now and then to prevent built up dust from staining the paper. A clean feather duster works best for this job but do not use any spray or polish.

Dust jackets can best be preserved by putting them in a non-adhesive protective dust jacket cover, such as those available from the library and archival supply companies listed in Appendix C. Do not to use tape or glue in affixing such a cover. Do not attempt to repair a broken book without professional advice, and never use tape or household glue on a book.

Delicate books which are quite valuable may justify your investment in a folding box or other protective container. Consult with you local bookbinder for a custom made box, or check in archival supply company catalogues for prefabricated ones.

Keep your fine books away from children, pets, and any other obvious source of potential damage. A book left on a coffee table may well incur a damaging dampstain from a guest who thought he was preserving your furniture by placing his drink on a book.

Exercise care in handling your books. Remove them from shelves carefully, without placing pressure on the spine. Never use bookmarks made of materials that may contain acid, such as uncoated paper, cloth, or leather, and never place an open book face down on a table. Keep paper clips, staples, and rubber bands away from your books, and never mark in them with a pen or highlighter. Do not write your name in fine books. If you must write in the vicinity of an open book, do so with a pencil in case you inadvertently mark in the book, and never use a book to bear down on when writing. Books which have unopened pages, that is pages which have not been cut open at the edge and therefore cannot be read, should be left that way if you can possible resist the urge to read them. If not, cut open the pages carefully with an extremely sharp knife.

Should I put bookplates in my books?

The answer to this question depends on your wishes for the future of your books. If you want to preserve as much of their value as possible, you should not mark them in any way, and this includes the pasting in of bookplates. Bookplates only add to the value of a book if they are from the library of the author or some other luminary. Assuming you are not such a figure, your bookplate will only negatively affect the book's future retail value.

If, however, you are interested in identifying your books for future generations and are not concerned about the possible effect on value, you may still want to put bookplates in your books. In any case, bookplates should be small, tastefully designed, made of acid free paper, and inobtrusively placed. Never paste a bookplate onto an illustrated endpaper or in such a way as to obscure any printing, and use an archival quality adhesive to attach your bookplates.

Should I treat leatherbound books with anything to preserve the leather?

There seem to be as many answers to this question as there are professional book restorers. Some recommend a certain kind of oil or mixture be rubbed on leather once a year or so, while others believe that leather lasts longest when left alone, especially if it is stored in the proper climate. This variety of answers is aggravated by the wide range of binding materials that fall under the heading "leather," as well as the variety of conditions that these materials might be found in.

More important than treating leather with any sort of oil is ensuring that leather books, like others, are kept in an environment that is neither too damp nor too dry. If you have leatherbound books which have begun to deteriorate or others which you feel would benefit from some sort of treatment, it is best to consult with a professional bookbinder or restorer who may be able to advise you on the care of your books. Rubbing anything on your books without professional advice is likely to do more harm than good.

Should I have deteriorating books repaired or rebound?

This difficult question must be answered only after taking into account several factors about your particular books. When properly done, the art of book restoration or rebinding can be both time consuming and expensive. There are few craftsmen qualified to deal with rare books, and all their work must be done by hand. In some cases, though, expert repair of a book can increase its value many times.

Before deciding to have a book restored you must consider many factors. The first and most important is: will the value of the book after its repair be as great or greater than the cost of that repair? Value may be measured in many ways. A family bible may have little resale value, but its sentimental worth may easily justify a $300 repair bill. In many cases, however, the cost of restoring a book will far exceed the value of the restored book. If you decide that salvaging a book is worth the cost involved, then proceed to the next question.

Should a book be repaired or restored or should a shabby volume be completely rebound? The answer to this question may determine the craftsman you choose for the job, the amount of money you spend, and what your finished book will look like. If the book is valuable and there is a reasonable chance of salvaging the original binding, restoration is the wiser course. Whenever the original components of a book can be saved, the book will have greater value than if they are replaced. Restoring a damaged binding is also less expensive than completely rebinding a book.

If your primary purpose for repairing a book is so it can be used on a regular basis or so it will look as beautiful as possible, or if the original binding is completely lacking or disintegrated, rebinding might be the proper course. Though it may detract somewhat from the market value of a rare volume, a new binding can be sturdier than a restored one, and can be made in any color or design you desire.

A bookbinder may offer you wide range of binding options, but, if you can afford it, consider having the book bound in a style similar to the original cover. There is something rather disconcerting about opening a plain cloth library binding and discovering a glorious job of seventeenth-century printing within. The details of restoring or rebinding a particular book should be discussed with the craftsman who will be doing the work. He will be able to describe your options and help you decide which are best suited for your book.

There is a satisfying feeling one gets from saving a book. Too often one must say "This is not worth it," but, when a tattered book comes along in which you can see potential value, no greater contribution can be made to the world of books than to wrap it up carefully and take it to an artist who can restore its former elegance.

How can I find a book restorer or binder?

The best place to begin the search for a book restorer or binder is at your local secondhand bookshop. If the proprietor there is unable to recommend a binder, you may ask other dealers with whom you have done business. The Guild of Bookworkers will send you a list of members residing in your state upon request, though this group does not endorse any particular craftsmen. The Center for Book Arts also maintains a list of book restorers, mostly in the New York area.

Because there are few professional hand binders, you may have to travel some distance or entrust your books to the US Mail or other shipping service in order to have them repaired or rebound.

Do I need to have my books appraised?

If you have a large number of valuable books you may want to have them appraised. Appraisals are done for many reasons from curiosity to tax purposes. If you purchased your books from reputable dealers, you probably have a good idea of their value. If you have collected for some time and have experience with the books in your field, you know as well as anyone what your books are worth. If, however, the books came to you through inheritance, gift, or discovery, or if, for legal reasons, you require a professional evaluation of your collection, an appraisal will be of some use to you.

In most cases, curiosity alone is not a sufficient justification for a professional appraisal. After all, by using the reference works described earlier in this book, you should be able to determine an approximate value of your books by yourself.

Appraisals are most often needed to evaluate estates, compute the details of insurance coverage, and calculate tax deductions for books donated to schools or libraries. Your individual situation will determine what type of appraisal you need—wholesale value, fair market value, or replacement value. Before having an appraisal conducted you will want to consult with both the appraiser and your lawyer, accountant, or insurance agent, whichever is appropriate, to decide which value applies to you.

Your local book dealer may be able to act as an appraiser for you, or recommend someone for the job. Appraisal services are also listed in most directories of dealers, including *American Book Trade Directory*. Before hiring an appraiser, obtain a statement of his qualifications and his fee schedule. Appraisal fees should be based on a hourly figure, not a percentage of the total appraisal. Hourly fees begin in the $50–$75 range, but may be much higher for specialized work.

An average book collector is unlikely to need the services of an appraiser except in unusual circumstances, especially if he keeps good records of what he has spent on books. Receipts or other records of expenditures on your collection may be used in many circumstances to avoid an expensive appraisal.

Should I insure my book collection?

Only your insurance agent can give you the answer to this question, but it is well worth asking. In some cases your collection may be covered by your homeowner's policy; in others you may require a separate rider to insure your books. In either case, it is important to keep a record of your books and their values in a safe place, preferably outside of your home. Keeping receipts from your book purchases can help ensure that the proper value is attributed to them should they be stolen or damaged.

How should I catalogue my collection?

Many collectors find it convenient to produce a shelf list of their collection. Such a list can assist with insurance claims should your collection be lost or damaged, and it can also help you avoid purchasing copies of books already in your collection. The form such a listing should take is dependent on your own personal style as well as the type of material you collect.

The personal computer can be an excellent tool for cataloguing your collection, since you can add items to your list without retyping the entire document. Another advantage of computer cataloguing is your ability to back up your list and avoid the risk of losing it. If you only wish to keep a list of items which can be printed out as you need it, a word processing program may fit your needs. If, on the other hand, you would like to be able to search your listing for particular items, or sort the list by date, author, or other factors, you may want to use a simple database program. There are some computer programs on the market designed especially for book collectors, but you should try these out before purchasing them. You may find that the software you are already using can fit your needs, and thus avoid any additional investment.

How can I find others who share my collecting interest?

By getting to know other collectors who share your interest you may open up opportunities to obtain new materials by buying, selling, and trading duplicate items with your peers. There are a number of societies devoted to the works of particular authors or other collecting fields, and most of these are listed in *The Encyclopaedia of Associations*, which you will probably find in the reference room of your local public or university library. Also, ask your local book dealer or a speciality dealer about getting in touch with others who share your interest.

How can I share my book collection with others?

For many collectors, one of the great joys of their pursuit is sharing it with other enthusiasts or creating new enthusiasts. If you wish to share your collection with people other than those you are able to lure into your living room, consider mounting an exhibition. Public libraries are often searching for books and other materials to fill their exhibition cases, and you may be able to work with your local public librarian to create a display from your books which will entertain and enlighten the library's patrons.

Investigate the possibility of mounting an exhibition in a school library, university rare book department, or even at your local bookshop. You may be surprised to find how many organizations in your community would be happy to help you share your book collection with the public. The enjoyment others get from your books will only add to your own enjoyment of collecting.

Are books a good investment?

The best reason to buy books is because you love them; however, prices of rare books have tended to rise at a pace slightly higher then the rate of inflation over the years, making them a fairly stable investment. Books will occasionally skyrocket in value. Tom Clancy's first novel, *The Hunt for Red October*, for instance, was published in 1984 in a small edition by an obscure publisher. A few years later, when Clancy was famous worldwide and the book had been made into a hit movie, the first edition was worth over $500. This is the exception rather than the rule, however, and books are certainly not an attractive commodity for speculative investors.

When considering the investment potential of books, keep in mind that, in most cases, you will purchase your books at a retail price and, should you wish to resell them, you will almost certainly do so at a wholesale price. The difference between these prices will often offset any capital gain you might have realized due to the increased value of your books.

You might make a profit by investing in books, but book buying should ultimately be motivated by love, not financial greed.

How can I sell books from my collection?

Even if you never want to divest yourself of your entire collection, there may be times when you want to sell a few books due to your changing interest or to your having purchased better copies. If the books are fairly ordinary, take them to your local bookshop where the proprietor will probably be willing to buy them or offer you credit towards future purchases. Most shops have minimum standards of condition and will probably not be interested in shabby volumes, book club editions, or ex-library books. Phone ahead to see what categories of books the shop buys.

If the books you wish to sell are of some significant value, you may wish to seek out a speciality dealer who can more easily evaluate and sell them and therefore may offer you a better price. If you bought the books from such a dealer, consider offering them back to the same dealer.

Whatever sort of dealer buys your books, bookselling, like any business, must be profitable in order to be maintained. To offer books to you, dealers must pay utilities, printing and mailing costs for catalogues, rent, employees' salaries, advertising, and many other expenses, while still making a living. For this reason, dealers rarely pay more than 50% of the retail price of a book when purchasing volumes for resale. This markup is similar to that in other retail establishments. If a dealer knows that he can sell your book right away, he may offer you more than 50%, but if the book is likely to be a slow seller, he will probably offer much less. Shops buying general used books are likely to pay less than 50% for stock, since the overhead to run a bookshop is greater than that to operate a speciality mail order firm.

If the price the dealer offers you is less than what you are willing to accept, politely decline and thank him for his time. Acting offended at what you believe is a low offer will only ensure that the dealer will not want to do business with you in the future.

If the books in question require the dealer to do a significant amount of research in order to make an offer, he may be within his rights to charge you for an appraisal if you refuse his offer. Be sure you understand the dealer's policy about such a situation before handing over your books.

What if I want to get rid of my entire collection?

The best method of disposing of your collection depends on the size and nature of the collection and your own wishes and needs.

If you wish to sell a collection that is significant in its field and includes fine copies of valuable books, you may want to consign it to an auction house. Auction houses will devote an entire sale to some extremely large and important collections. The advantages of selling your books at auction are the chance to have the price decided on the open market by competitive bidding, the opportunity to see your books professionally catalogued, and the relatively low cost to you. Most auction houses charge between 10% and 30% of the hammer price to the consignor, depending on the price of the lot. The disadvantage of selling at auction is that auction houses are only interested in fairly valuable books. In order to be profitable, auction catalogues must include lots priced in the hundreds and thousands of dollars. While smaller auction houses are willing to take on less expensive lots, if your collection consists primarily of $50 books, an auction house may not be your best avenue for selling.

If you know of a dealer whose speciality covers your field of collecting, consider selling or consigning the collection to him. If your collection is unified around a subject or author, the dealer may be willing to devote an entire catalogue to it, giving you a written record of your collection. Some dealers are willing to take collections on consignment, especially if the purchase price would be very high. This may work to your advantage, as the dealer could offer you a larger percentage of sales since he would not have to risk any financial outlay beyond the cost of the catalogue. On the other hand, books that remained unsold would still be yours. An outright sale to a dealer would give you money in hand immediately and you would not have to wait and wonder how much you are going to get.

If you are more concerned with preserving the integrity of your collection than making money, consider donating it to a library. The cost of adding a book to a library collection can be as much as $50, however, even if the book is donated. For this reason, some libraries may not want your collection, and few are likely to want all of your books. When searching for a library for your books, consider how the collection might be used. A collection of performing arts books, for instance, might go to a school of the arts, or a railroading collection may find a place at an engineering school. When donating books to a library, be sure you understand exactly what the library will do with your books. Imagine your reaction if a few months later you see books which you thought were headed to a rare book room on the table at the annual library book sale!

Finally, if your collection is eclectic or composed primarily of inexpensive books, you may wish to consider donating it to a library sale or other charity organization sale. Elementary and high school libraries, which typically have very small acquisitions budgets, also appreciate contributions of books.

Afterword:
The Ten Commandments
of
Book Collecting

There is a lot of information in this book, presented, I hope, in a clear and understandable format. If you want to remember only one page, though, make it this one. When I try to boil down all my advice on book collecting to ten tidbits, I come up with these.

1) Buy books that you love—all other considerations are secondary.
2) Set limits without limiting yourself. True, it's an oxymoron, but try to gain focus without losing imagination.
3) Be discriminating. Condition is the most important factor in the value of a book.
4) Invest in a few basic reference books. They will pay for themselves many times over.
5) Learn. Read reference books, dealers' catalogues, and anything about books you can get your hands on.
6) Be prepared. Bookshops surface in the most unlikely of places, so don't get caught without your want list and any other guides you may need.
7) Buy it. I have never met a collector who regretted making a particular purchase. I have met hundreds who regretted not making one.
8) Take care of your books. Treat them with respect.
9) Get to know the people. Dealers and collectors are your greatest resource for books and friendship. Cultivate relationships with them.
10) Share. The greatest joy of collecting is sharing your passion and your books with others.

Grading a Book's Condition

Every collector has his own standards of condition and every dealer has his own way of describing condition. A book catalogued as "fine" by one dealer may qualify as only "very good" to another. When a book is in less than fine condition, the dealer describing it should enumerate any significant faults, a practice which gives the potential purchaser a much better picture of the book's condition than merely the letters "VG." Different types of books may be graded by different criteria, too. "Fine" may be used to describe a copy of an eighteenth-century book while a recent novel in similar condition might rate only "very good." When describing the condition of a book with a dust jacket, the book's condition is noted first. Thus a fine book in a very good dust jacket would be described "F/VG." The following guidelines for describing a book's condition are quite general but also widely accepted in the book business. A familiarity with them should prevent any major surprises when ordering from a dealer's catalogue.

Very Fine (VF)—The highest grade of book condition. The terms "mint" or "as new" are sometimes used in describing books but mint is more properly applied to coins, and "as new" is simply less descriptive than "very fine" since a new book may have some faults. A very fine book has no flaws whatsoever nor does its dust jacket. The book is crisp and clean and has probably never been read. The dust jacket is not price-clipped, smudged or adorned with a price sticker (unless the publisher issued it that way). The only acceptable mark is a lightly pencilled price and bookseller's code on the first page.

Fine (F)—Nearly as good as "very fine." A fine book may have been read once or more, but by readers who protected the dust jacket, took care not to put stress on the spine, and did not handle pages with dirty fingers. A fine book has no discernible flaws, but may lack the pristine appearance of a very fine copy.

Very Good (VG)—This is the most common grade of collectible book. Most books on a collector's shelves and in a dealer's catalogue are likely to be very good, and this condition is acceptable to most collectors. A very good book will have no serious defects, but will show some minor signs of wear to either the book or the dust jacket or both. The book will probably have been read several times, but will not have any major soiling, tears, or markings. Many dealers will describe minor flaws in a book (a small tear in the dust jacket, some discoloration of the endpapers) and then add the designation "otherwise very good."

Good (G)—When asked what "good" means, most dealers will say, "it means not very good." In fact, many collectors will not purchase "good" books unless they are desperate for a particular title. "Good" books have one or more major flaws, which should be described by anyone offering such a book for sale. "Good" books must be complete, however. Acceptable flaws for a good book include tears or chips in the dust jacket, water damage to the cover or pages, soiling or light marking within the book, and many other similar faults.

Fair or Poor—Books in fair or poor condition (poor is worse but both are bad) are not sought after by collectors unless they are extremely rare. Such books may have loose or detached bindings (the latter would be described as a binding copy), ink underlining or highlighting of text, missing illustrations, or severely torn and chipped dust jackets. A copy which is in fair or poor condition but in which the text is still complete and readable is called a reading copy.

Glossary of Terms Not Covered in the Text

Backstrip The cloth or leather covering the *spine* of a book.

Bands/raised bands The bands of a book are pieces of cord onto which the *signatures* are sewn. If these cords are thick enough to cause horizontal ridges in the *backstrip* they are called raised bands. Some contemporary books have imitation raised bands to give the illusion of a fine binding.

Blurb A promotional statement about a book printed on the dust jacket and sometimes written by a famous author or other recognizable figure.

Boards The covers of a book, so called because at one time they were made from wooden boards.

Broadside A single sheet of paper printed on one side.   Today broadsides are often printed by private presses as a means to publish limited editions of poems.. In times past broadsides were often advertisements for performances, auctions, or other events.

Cancel A leaf which is inserted into a book after it has been bound.

Usually a cancel leaf is glued in to replace a leaf on which some error has been printed.

Chapbook An inexpensive and widely marketed style of book popular in the 17th, 18th, and early 19th centuries. Chapbooks are usually 8, 16, or 32 pages; fairly small in format; and bound in paper wrappers. The content was most often religious texts and children's stories.

Conjugate leaves *Leaves* which are part of the same sheet of paper and are still attached. Determining if two leaves are conjugate can be difficult without disbinding a book.

Deckled edge The untrimmed, uneven edge of handmade paper used in some fine books. Some machine made papers imitate this deckling to give the illusion of handmade paper.

Endpapers The pages which connect the contents of a book to its cover. A book has four endpapers; the front and back paste-downs, which are pasted to the inside of the book's covers, and the front and back free endpapers which are the first and last pages of the book.

Errata slip A small slip of paper *tipped* or bound into the front of a book which describes errors in the text. Errata slips are fragile and are often lacking from books in which they were originally present. Therefore, the presence of an errata slip will usually increase the value of a book.

Extra-illustrated A copy of a book which has had additional illustrations beyond those included in the regular edition bound in. The extra illustrations are sometimes original works of art.

Facsimile A precise reproduction of a book, usually one of some historical significance. Most facsimiles clearly state that they are reproductions, but some which strive to reproduce not only the original printing but the binding and paper as well can be difficult to differentiate from the originals which they copy.

Flyleaf A blank leaf at the beginning or end of a book, including the free *endpapers*.

Fore-edge painting A scene painted on the edges of the pages of a book in such a way that the painting is visible only when the pages of the book are fanned out. Such paintings are generally found on 18th and 19th-century books, though some were executed years after the publication date of the books on which they appear. A double fore-edge painting reveals two different scenes—depending on in which direction the pages are fanned.

Foxing A rust colored, spotty discoloration of paper, often seen in 19th-century books, caused by deposits of minerals and other impurities in the paper.

Frontispiece An illustration printed on the page facing the title page of a book.

Gathering or signature A group of pages created by folding a single large sheet of paper several times. Most books have signatures of 4, 8, 16, or 32 pages and in well bound books each signature is stitched into the binding. Books in poor condition sometimes have loose signatures.

Half title or bastard title Generally the first printed page of a book, it contains the title, sometimes abbreviated, and no other information.

Half leather or quarter leather A book is described as quarter bound in leather if only the *spine* is covered in leather. A half leather binding is one in which the spine and the corners of the covers are covered in leather.

Head and foot/tail of spine The head of the *spine* is the top and the foot or tail of the spine is the bottom.

Headband/footband Small pieces of cloth at the top and bottom of the *spine*. In older books they strengthened the binding, in contemporary books they are primarily decorative, the headband being much more common than the footband.

Hinge The joining of a book's cover and the body of the book inside the front and rear covers. Older books are often found with cracked or broken hinges, causing the binding to be either loose or completely detached.

Inner dentelle In a leatherbound book, the small strip of leather that runs around the inside of the covers. So called when it is decorated with *tooling or stamping*.

Joint The external joining of the covers of a book to its *spine*.

Leaf A single piece of paper in a book. A leaf consists of two pages, one page being printed on each side of the leaf.

Marbled paper Paper that is decorated in a marbled pattern. Often used in bindings or as *endpapers* for fine books.

Pictorial boards *Boards* which are decorated with illustrations. Often seen on children's books.

Prelims or front matter Printed material in a book which precedes the body of the text. Generally includes the *half-title*, title page, copyright information, the table of contents, acknowledgments, and the dedication.

Provenance The history of ownership of a particular copy of a book. If a book has been owned by a famous individual its provenance may contribute to its value.

Rebacked A rebacked book has had its *backstrip* replaced.

Recto The front of a *leaf* or a page on the right hand side of a book.

Sizes Book sizes are based on the practice of folding a large sheet of paper to create several pages. A traditional sized sheet which is folded once to create four pages yields a quarto (4to) sized book, a sheet folded twice to create eight pages yields an octavo (8vo) sized book, and so on. The most commonly used book size designations and their approximate heights in inches are:

Miniature	3" or less
48mo	under 4"

Trigesimosecundo (32mo)	4" to 5"
Vigesimoquarto (24mo)	5" to 6"
Sextodecimo (16mo)	6" to 7"
Duodecimo (12mo)	7" to 8"
Octavo (8vo)	about 8" to 11"
Quarto (4to)	11" to 13"
Folio	over 13"
Elephant Folio	over 23"
Double Elephant Folio	over 25"

Spine The portion of a book which connects the front and back covers. The spine is usually printed with the title of the book and often the author and publisher as well.

Stamping/tooling/blind-stamping Stamped or tooled decoration or lettering on the cover of a book which is created by a die cut metal stamp, in the case of machine bindings, or either a stamp or hand tools, in the case of hand bindings. Stamping is often colored with foil or ink. When it is not colored it is blind stamping.

Tipped in A tipped-in *leaf* is one which has been glued into the book after it has been bound. *Cancel* leaves are usually tipped-in.

Top edge gilt (TEG) or all edges gilt (AEG) A book on which the top edges of the pages, or all the edges, have been covered with a very thin layer of gold. In contemporary books the edges are sometimes covered with gold ink in imitation of true gilt. Top edges are also often stained with ink. The practice of gilding or staining the edges originated to keep dust out of the pages.

Vellum A fine type of leather similar to parchment which is prepared from the skin of a lamb, calf, or kid. Vellum is smooth and a creamy white color and is most often used in binding, though sometimes used for the pages of a book.

Verso The back of a *leaf* or the page on the left hand side of a book.

Wrappers Paper binding of a book. Paperback books, pamphlets, and chapbooks are all described as being bound in wrappers.

Sources & Further Reading

Hundreds of bibliographies and price guides have been published over the years, some general in nature, others highly focused. The following list covers books and periodicals which will be of use to the majority of book collectors and which will lead you to more specialized reference works. Books marked with a † are priced over $100 per volume, and I recommend that you use copies at a public or academic library. Books marked with an * may be ordered directly from the publisher. Other books I recommend you order through a new book store.

Periodicals:

AB Bookman's Weekly. Weekly trade journal of the out-of-print book market. Includes articles on collecting and other topics, bookfair calendar, and classified advertisements of books wanted and for sale by dealers. *AB* also publishes a yearbook with advertisements and a directory of dealers. Information: P.O. Box AB, Clifton , NJ, 07015.

Antiquarian Book Monthly. Monthly magazine with articles about authors, books, and collections as well as an extensive book review section, auction and bookfair calendar, and other information on the book trade. Information: ABMR Publications Ltd., Jubilee House, The Oaks, Ruslip, Middlesex, HA4 7LF, England.

The Book Collector. Quarterly journal of scholarly content of interest to book collectors and bibliographers. Information: The Collector, Ltd., 68 Neal St., Covent Garden, London, WC2H 9PA.

Book Quote. Small publication consisting primarily of classified advertisements of books wanted and for sale. Also includes listings of recently published catalogues. Information: The Spoon River Press, 2319-C West Rohman Ave., Peoria, IL, 61604-5072.

Book Source Monthly. A small publication which is especially useful for its comprehensive listings of bookfairs and auctions. Also includes advertisements (including classifieds), short articles, lists of recently published catalogues, and seasonal listings of open bookshops. Information: P.O. Box 567, Cazenovia, NY, 13035-0567.

Firsts: Collecting Modern First Editions. Glossy magazine which covers the field of collecting modern literature. Includes bookfair calendar, auction and catalogue highlights, articles on particular authors and types of books with priced checklists, and advertisements. Information: P.O. Box 16945, North Hollywood, CA, 91615.

MFE Collectors' Bookline. An expensive but informative newsletter directed at collectors of modern first editions. Includes details of upcoming books and schedules of readings and signings by current authors. Information: P.O. Box 150119, San Rafael, CA, 94915.

Price Guides:

†*American Book Prices Current.* Published annually by Bancroft-Parman, Inc. (P.O. Box 1236, Washington, CT, 06793). Records auction results for autographs, manuscripts, books, broadsides, maps, and charts. Covers items selling for at least $50 at major auction houses in the United States, Europe, Australia, and Monaco. Also includes addresses for auction houses listed.

†*Bookman's Price Index* edited by Daniel F. McGrath. Published on a regular basis by Gale Research, Inc. (835 Penobscot Bldg., Detroit, MI, 48226-4094). Compiled from dealer's catalogues. In-

cludes separate sections for association copies, fine bindings, and fore-edge paintings, plus a listing of dealers whose catalogues are used.

Book Prices: Used and Rare edited by Edward N. Zempel and Linda A. Verkler. Published by The Spoon River Press (2319-C West Rohman Ave., Peoria, IL, 61604-5072). The first volume of this projected annual series was published in 1993 and concentrated on books in the $20–$300 range. Though still expensive, this guide is far more affordable than other annually published volumes.

Collected Books The Guide to Values by Allen and Patricia Ahearn. Published by Putnam (200 Madison Ave., New York, NY, 10016). An excellent one-volume source for book prices, especially modern first editions and other popular areas of collecting.

Hancer's Price Guide to Paperback Books by Kevin Hancer. Published by Wallace-Homestead Book Co. (201 King of Prussia Road, Radnor, PA, 19089).

Mandeville's Used Book Price Guide edited by Richard C. Collins. Published every five years (new edition 1994) by Price Guide Publishers (P.O. Box 82525, Kenmore, WA, 98208). Prices compiled from dealer catalogues. Includes many less expensive books not listed in other guides.

Modern First Editions by Joseph Connolly. Published by Macdonald and Co., Publishers, Ltd. Available in the USA from Trans-Atlantic Publishers, Inc. (311 Bainbridge St., Philadelphia, PA, 19147). Consists of priced checklists for the most collected modern authors with an emphasis on British writers and editions.

The Official Price Guide—Paperbacks by Jon Warren. Published by House of Collectibles (201 E. 50th St., New York, NY, 10022).

The Price Guide to Autographs by George Sanders, Helen Sanders, and Ralph Roberts. Published by Wallace-Homestead Book Co. (201 King of Prussia Road, Radnor, PA, 19089). Gives prices for autographs, letters, and documents in all fields. Illustrated with a sampling of facsimile autographs.

Other Useful Reference Books:

†*American Book Trade Directory*. Published annually by R. R. Bowker (121 Chanlon Road, New Providence, NJ, 07974). Includes geographical listings of new and used booksellers in the USA as well as book wholesalers, auctions houses dealing in books, and book appraisers.

†*Books In Print*. Published annually by R. R. Bowker (121 Chanlon Road, New Providence, NJ, 07974). Includes listings by title, author, and subject of books currently available from most American publishers.

**Buy Books Where, Sell Books Where* compiled by Ruth E. Robinson. Published biannually by Ruth E. Robinson Books (Route 7, Box 162A, Morgantown, WV, 26505). Includes geographical and specialty listings of dealers in secondhand and collectible books.

The Care of Fine Books by Jane Greenfield. Published by Lyons & Burford, Publishers (31 W. 21st St., New York, NY, 10010). An illustrated guide to storing, handling, and caring for fine books, with advice on restoration and rebinding.

†*Encyclopedia of Associations*. Published by Gale Research (835 Penobscot Bldg., Detroit, MI, 48226-4094). Includes listings for a variety of literary associations, including those devoted to a particular field or the works of a particular author.

**First Editions: A Guide to Identification* edited by Edward N. Zempel and Linda A. Verkler. Published by The Spoon River Press (2319-C West Rohman Ave., Peoria, IL, 61604-5072). The most comprehensive and in-depth guide to identifying first editions. A must for any serious collector.

**A Pocket Guide to the Identification of First Editions & Points of Issue* compiled by Bill McBride. Published by McBride Publisher (585 Prospect Ave., West Hartford, CT, 06105). Two inexpensive booklets which will help you identify first editions of collectible books.

Organizations:

Antiquarian Booksellers' Association of America (ABAA). Organization of major antiquarian booksellers in the US. Membership list available upon request (send business envelope with 3 oz. of postage). 50 Rockefeller Center, New York, NY, 10020. (212) 757-9535.

Center for Book Arts. Dedicated to the traditional crafts of bookmaking and binding. Will provide lists of book restorers in the New York area on request. 626 Broadway, New York, NY, 10012. (212) 460-9768.

Supplies:

The following are library and archival supply houses which provide archival storage supplies, dust jacket covers, and other materials of interest to book collectors.

Archivart. 301 Veterans Blvd., Rutherford, NJ, 07070. (800-631-0193).
Brodart Company. 1609 Memorial Ave., Williamsport, PA, 17705. (800) 233-8467.
Conservation Resources International, Inc. 8000-H Forbes Place, Springfield, VA, 22151. (800-634-6932).
Demco. Box 7488, Madison, WI, 53707. (800) 356-1200.
The Hollinger Company. P.O. Box 8360, Fredericksburg, VA, 22404. (800-634-0491).
Light Impressions. 439 Monroe Ave., Rochester, NY, 14603-0940. (800-828-6216).
University Products, Inc. 517 Main St., P.O. Box 101, Holyoke, MA, 01041-0101. (800-628-1912, in MA 800-336-4847).

Index

CHARLIE LOVETT has been in the collectible book business as both dealer and collector for nearly a decade. He has worked in bookstores, done projects for rare book libraries, and owned and operated an antiquarian bookshop. He has also lectured on books and authors in England and the US at literary societies, book clubs, schools, libraries, and the Smithsonian Institution. He has co-written one bibliography and served as authorial assistant on two others.

JONATHAN DIXON is a graduate student in Philosophy at the University of North Dakota. His first illustrated book, Lewis Carroll's *The Hunting of the Snark*, was published in 1992 by the Lewis Carroll Society of North America.